A BLUE BANNER
BIOGRAPHY

Ice Cube

Tamra Orr

P.O. Box 196
Hockessin, Delaware 19707
Visit us on the web: www.mitchelllane.com
Comments? email us: mitchelllane@mitchelllane.com

Mitchell Lane PUBLISHERS

Printing   1   2   3   4   5   6   7   8   9

Blue Banner Biographies

Alan Jackson	Alicia Keys	Allen Iverson
Ashanti	Ashlee Simpson	Ashton Kutcher
Avril Lavigne	Bernie Mac	Beyoncé
Bow Wow	Britney Spears	Christina Aguilera
Christopher Paul Curtis	Clay Aiken	Condoleezza Rice
Daniel Radcliffe	Derek Jeter	Eminem
Eve	50 Cent	Gwen Stefani
Ice Cube	Jamie Foxx	Ja Rule
Jay-Z	Jennifer Lopez	J. K. Rowling
Jodie Foster	Justin Berfield	Kate Hudson
Kelly Clarkson	Kenny Chesney	Lance Armstrong
Lindsay Lohan	Mariah Carey	Mario
Mary-Kate and Ashley Olsen	Melissa Gilbert	Michael Jackson
Miguel Tejada	Missy Elliott	Nelly
Orlando Bloom	P. Diddy	Paris Hilton
Peyton Manning	Queen Latifah	Rita Williams-Garcia
Ritchie Valens	Ron Howard	Rudy Giuliani
Sally Field	Selena	Shirley Temple
Tim McGraw	Usher	

Library of Congress Cataloging-in-Publication Data
Orr, Tamara.
       Ice Cube/ by Tamara Orr.
              p. cm. — (Blue banner biographies)
       Includes bibliographical references and index.
       ISBN 1-58415-517-5 (library bound: alk. paper)
       1. Ice Cube (Musician)—Juvenile literature. 2. Rap musicians—United States—Biography—
Juvenile literature. 3. Actors—United States—Biography—Juvenile literature.
       I. Title. II. Series: Blue banner biography.
       ML3930.I34077 2007
       782. 421649092—dc22
       [B]   2006014799
ISBN-10: 1-58415-517-5   ISBN-13: 9781584155171

ABOUT THE AUTHOR: Tamra Orr is a full-time writer and author living in the Pacific Northwest. She has written more than 50 educational books for children and families, including *The Dawn of Aviation: The Story of the Wright Brothers* and *Orlando Bloom* for Mitchell Lane Publishers. She is a regular writer for more than 50 national magazines and a dozen standardized testing companies. Orr is mother to four and life partner to Joseph.

PHOTO CREDITS: Cover: Frederick M. Brown/Getty Images; p. 4 Gary Gershoff/WireImage.com; p. 7 Fitzroy Barrett/Globe Photos; p. 10 Kirby Lee/WireImage.com; p. 14 Arnold Turner WireImage.com; p. 18 Frederick M. Brown/Getty Images; p. 22 AccuSoft Inc./Getty Images; p. 26 Stephen Shugerman/Getty Images; p. 28 Vince Bucci/Getty Images

PUBLISHER'S NOTE: The following story has been thoroughly researched, and to the best of our knowledge represents a true story. While every possible effort has been made to ensure accuracy, the publisher will not assume liability for damages caused by inaccuracies in the data, and makes no warranty on the accuracy of the information contained herein. This story has not been authorized or endorsed by Ice Cube.

CONTENTS

Ice Cube raps to the crowd in the intimate setting of B.B. King Blues Club and Grill in New York City. He has been writing rap songs since 1983, when he was 14 years old.

"You Write One,
I Write One"

*I*t was another typical day at school. Fourteen-year-old O'Shea Jackson was sitting in typing class, keeping a close eye on the clock and wishing it would move faster. Somehow time seemed to slow down whenever he was sitting at a desk. Despite his restlessness, he was a pretty good student, keeping a B average on his report cards. He liked drawing, math, and sports the best. Ninth-grade typing was just too dull.

Just then he heard a familiar voice. "Hey, O'Shea!" called Kiddo, one of his best friends. "Have you ever written a rap song?"

O'Shea shook his head and then sat back, deep in thought. No, he hadn't written one. Why hadn't he, though? He loved rap and hip-hop music, of course. He had from the very first moment he heard the song

"Rapper's Delight" by the Sugarhill Gang. Years later, he would still remember that day quite clearly. It was 1979 and he was ten years old. He had gotten out of school early to go to a dentist appointment. His uncle was driving him to it. Since there was no radio in the car, O'Shea slipped in one of his uncle's cassette tapes. "Rapper's Delight" began to play, and he was completely entranced by it. He had never heard any song performed like that before. "I listened to it the whole way to the dentist," he recalls. "I thought about it while I was at the dentist's, left the dentist's playing the song and I wanted to borrow the tape."

> O'Shea slipped in one of his uncle's cassette tapes. "Rapper's Delight" played, and he was entranced by it.

From that day, O'Shea knew that he had discovered the best music in the world. He listened to the radio and just waited for another rap song to come on.

So, why hadn't he thought of writing his own rap song? He was sure he could. Kiddo had the right idea. "We had some time on our hands, so he said let's write a rap," says O'Shea. "I told him, you write one, I write one and we'll see which one comes out better . . . and I won. From then on, I never stopped. I had been a rap fan but I had never thought about doing it!"

At fourteen, many teenagers think they are capable of almost anything. In the case of O'Shea Jackson,

Ice Cube attends the movie premiere of Polar Express *in Hollywood with his wife, Kimberly (right), their daughter (middle), and two of their three sons. As a parent, he advises others: "Never forget how it was to be their age — that is the key, and remember what you went through. Remember what you thought of the world."*

already known to many as Ice Cube, it was true. It would not be long before his first rap song was followed by countless others. It also was not long before he met the very person who could help him get started in a music career he had only dreamed of.

From Juice to Cube

*T*he actor and singer known as Ice Cube started out with an entirely different name. O'Shea Jackson was born on June 15, 1969, in Crenshaw, a neighborhood in South Central Los Angeles. He was Hosea and Doris Jackson's fourth child, joining one brother and two sisters. When Doris went to name her new son, she thought of a young, handsome African-American football player that she often saw on television. His name was O.J. Simpson. She softened the sound, spelled it out, and named her son O'Shea.

Both Hosea and Doris worked for the University of California at Los Angeles (UCLA). Hosea was a machinist and groundskeeper. Doris was a clerk. Both of them wanted the best for all of their children. The neighborhood they lived in made this more than a little challenging. It was known for terrible drug problems and high crime rates. The biggest issue that worried them, however, was gangs. There was a constant fear that the Jackson children would fall into the trap of violent and destructive gang life. The family had already lost one child, Cube's half-sister, who died in 1981. They wanted to make sure the others stayed safe. As Cube recalls, "I was just 12, so that was my wake-up call in life, and what it is really about, you know. A lot of people who were deep into the gangs . . . didn't have fathers or older brothers to set them straight. But I had that; I have an older brother and a father. My brother had been through all of that [stuff], so he was like, 'Man, you don't have to do that.'"

Cube credits his family, and especially his father and brother Clyde, for pointing him in the most positive direction. "[My father] was there," he says. "He kept me on the right track. You don't realize that until you see other people who grew up without fathers, and how their lives turn out." He adds, "My father just gave me the freedom to do what I wanted. He would teach me things at home and [let me] see if it worked." About Clyde, he says, "My brother is nine years older than myself. I looked up to both of them because they were always available, always there with anything I needed to help

> *Cube credits his family, especially his father and brother Clyde, for pointing him in the most positive direction.*

Ice Cube dribbles up the court during the 2005 NBA Entertainment League Charity Basketball Game, hosted by the Los Angeles Clippers. The game benefited inner-city youth. Although never a professional athlete, Ice Cube has played football and basketball from a young age.

me get through the day, you know, living in South Central Los Angeles and trying not to get caught in all the traps it had."

Like the man he was named for, Cube liked to play football from a young age. He played on the Pop Warner Leagues for five years. He was usually a fullback or an outside linebacker. His abilities on the field earned him his first nickname: Juice, once again after football superstar O.J. Simpson. "My brother, to this day, still calls me Juice because of the way I played football on our street," recalls Cube. "I was fast, could catch and run and since my real name is O'Shea Jackson, my initials are O.J." Cube also played basketball at the local YMCA.

It was not his sports ability that earned him the nickname that would become his professional name, however. Instead it was his desire to impress the young ladies. He would stroll up to his older brother's girlfriends and try to flirt with them. He apparently thought he was so cool that his brother named him Ice Cube. The name stuck. From then on, everyone except his parents would call him Ice Cube. One day, it would be one of the most recognized names in music and film.

> *Cube liked to play football from a young age. He played on the Pop Warner Leagues for five years.*

Wrong School, Right Music

Middle school can be tough. The days of childhood are falling behind and young adulthood is just around the corner. For Ice Cube, these years were particularly difficult. His best friend, a boy named Randy, had decided to go to the new Hawthorne Christian Middle School after his mother had gotten brochures saying how wonderful it was. The boys hated the idea of being separated. The Jacksons finally agreed to send their youngest to Hawthorne as well. Their intentions were good. They simply did not know the story behind the school's campaign.

Hawthorne Middle School was trying to integrate their student population. In order to balance out the number of white people, African-American students were being brought in by buses. As Cube remembers it, "I got bussed to school; my mom didn't want me in our neighborhood because they knew the neighborhood [ate] up so many youngsters. And so they figured, yeah, we'll bus him off to school and give him a better chance at an education, stand and focus on education and not get into neighborhood school stuff.

"So, I went up there and basically they didn't want us out there," he explains. "You know, a lot of kids got bussed from the inner city to the valley and the community, the faculty really didn't want us out there. Some of them could disguise that and kind of do their job, but some of them couldn't. Some of them would let you know in so many ways. You know, so, I kind of faced a little bit [of racial discrimination] every day." Eventually, the Jacksons pulled their son out of Hawthorne and put him into William Howard Taft School instead. It was there that he wrote his very first rap song.

After that, Cube was hooked. He kept writing, and when he was only sixteen, he teamed up with another student, Tony Wheatob, better known to his friends as Sir Jinx. Together they formed a group that they first called Stereo Crew and then C.I.A., which stood for "Cru' in Action." They rehearsed in Sir Jinx's garage. One day, Sir Jinx introduced Cube to Jinx's cousin, who happened to

> *Together they formed a group that they first called Stereo Crew and then C.I.A., which stood for "Cru' in Action."*

have a connection to a disc jockey named Dr. Dre. The two boys rapped one of Cube's songs for the DJ and he liked it. Soon, the boys were performing in local roller rinks and nightclubs. Much of their act was made up of popular songs on the radio rewritten to include a lot of swearing and a stronger beat. They put their songs on a tape and sold it out of the back of their cars. As Cube recalls, "When that started catching on, we starting making mixed tapes. We would rap on what was going on in the neighborhood and they were selling."

In the late 1980s, C.I.A. merged with Dr. Dre's band, World Class Wreckin' Cru. The group included a new singer named Eric Wright, known as Eazy-E. Cube wrote

In his musical and acting career, Ice Cube has collaborated with many other successful rappers, including Snoop Dogg (above), Dr. Dre, Eazy-E, and Ice-T.

a song for another rap group called Boyz N the Hood, but the group did not care for it. Dr. Dre had already paid for 10,000 twelve-inch singles to be made of the song, so he and Eazy-E and Cube recorded it themselves. They had a song but they didn't have a name. Cube remembers the day they thought of it. "One day Dre and Eazy picked me up in the van and they was like — 'you know what we gonna call the group?' I was like, what? And they said, 'Niggaz with Attitude.' . . . [That] sounded like a plan." NWA was born.

At the same time that Cube was spending his evening hours rapping and recording, he was also holding down a job parking cars in downtown Los Angeles. He hated the job. "Getting up at 4:30 A.M. wasn't all bad," he says. "By getting out of the hood early, I could avoid the embarrassment of my polyester tie, polyester pants and starched white shirt; it wasn't fashion . . . it was an *embarrassment*."

> *Just as NWA thought they might have something important going, Cube surprised them by announcing he was going to college.*

In 1987, just as NWA thought they might have something important going, Cube surprised them by announcing that he was going to college. "The rap game wasn't looking too solid at that time," he explains, "so I decided to go ahead and go to school." His parents wanted their youngest son to have something to fall back on in case the music career did not work out. Cube enrolled in the Phoenix Institute of Technology in Arizona. "I got into drafting because I was the kind of kid who, if I liked Magic Johnson, I would draw pictures of Magic Johnson," says Cube. "But I think that job would've been too boring for me. I'm not a nine-to-five kind of cat."

During his year in school, Cube earned a diploma in Architectural Drafting and Design. In between classes, he kept writing song lyrics for the group. He kept in touch with them and was shocked to hear that they were selling thousands of copies of their singles. "I'd get calls from them, 'We're about to fly to Chicago, then we fly to Atlanta.' And I'm asking, 'How much you all making?' 'They're gonna give us $10,000 a show.' And here I have six months of school left! That was the worst year of my life," admits Cube. "My dreams were leaving me behind."

Cube earned a diploma in Architectural Drafting and Design. In between classes, he kept writing song lyrics for the group.

When the year finally ended, Cube returned to his world of rap and rhythm. It was just in time, too. NWA was about to set the world of music on fire.

From Compton to Stardom

Now that the NWA was back together, it was time to release a full album that would catch the attention of rap and hip-hop fans everywhere. In 1988, and in what Cube describes as "reality-based gangster rap," the NWA put out *Straight Outta Compton.* (Compton is a city south of Los Angeles that is notorious for having the highest violent crime rate in California.) In the years since its release, the power of this music has not faded. In fact, many experts consider the album to be one of the most influential pieces of music since the beginning of rap in 1970.

Straight Outta Compton was, by no means, an easy piece of music to listen to. Although it had the driving, steady beat that rap music is known for, it also had lyrics that definitely required "parental advisory" stickers. While rap music fans loved it, many reviewers were shocked and bothered by its violent and crude lyrics. Cube says, "We told it like it was in our neighborhoods. Most of the people who sit around asking themselves why we are so angry have never set foot in Compton." In another interview, he says, "Everybody had that record and everybody knew about that record. [It] has had [a bigger] impact on rap music than any other album to this day. . . . We opened the door where you can say exactly what you really want

Ice Cube's talent and determination took him out of Compton and, after years of hard work, to megastardom.

to say without having to sugar-coat, without having to hold back." Despite the controversy over the lyrics, *Straight Outta Compton* went platinum (at least 1 million copies sold) in less than three months—and that was without any of the songs being played on the radio.

The songs on this album were certainly angry and loud. They looked squarely at unpleasant issues like racism, drug addiction, and more. According to Cube, however, that is what rap music is about. "What does it mean to be a rapper?" he says. "It's a way to get people's attention. In rhyming and rapping, you're bragging, boasting, it's about ego, bravado, being witty and clever and ironic. A lot of people say hip-hop is focused on being angry . . . that's how it started. . . . The essence of rap is to beat your chest." The music spotlights important issues that otherwise might be overlooked or ignored. "They [rap records] were done to inform, to bring to light things that aren't talked about enough. They weren't done out of being controversial. They were done because no one was saying it, nobody's gonna say it, and nobody's gonna say it like I'm gonna say it."

As big a success as the NWA's album was, however, it was not enough to hold the group together. In 1989,

Straight Outta Compton went platinum in less than three months—without the songs being played on the radio.

Cube left the group. He was not happy with the amount of money he had been paid. He decided it was time for him to go out on his own, so he moved from California to New York City. As he put it, "You've got to have the determination, the talent and you have to recognize opportunities and seize the moment."

In 1990, Cube proved that he knew how to seize the moment. He released his first solo album. It was called *AmeriKKKa's Most Wanted*. It went gold in ten days and platinum in three months. That same year he was offered his first real movie role. A film was being made called *Boyz N the Hood*, based on the song he had written. He was asked to star in it as a character named Doughboy. He played the role so well that it was not long before other movie offers began coming in. It looked like life had a few new opportunities for Ice Cube.

He released his first solo album, called AmeriKKKa's Most Wanted. It went gold in ten days and platinum in three months.

The Roles Keep Coming

The 1990s were busy, successful years for Ice Cube. As soon as he would release an album, he'd star in another movie. His music continued to offend some people. He still talked about topics and used language that pleased his listeners but upset their parents.

He made many music videos. He released *Death Certificate* and *Predator* with his usual style of rhythm, rap, and raging. Some radio stations refused to play his songs because of the lyrics. A few stores would not put up his posters, either. Despite that, *Predator* was the first rap album to enter the Billboard charts at number one.

In between making the albums, Cube starred in the movie *Trespass* along with fellow rapper Ice-T. He played an assistant to a crime lord. His character had a very hot temper. Since so many of his roles required him to look angry, hostile, or unhappy, the Ice Cube scowl, at once menacing and tough, became a familiar sight to moviegoers.

The early nineties also turned this growing star into a family man. In 1990, his first son, O'Shea Jackson Jr., was born. In 1992, he married Kimberly Jackson. Over the next several years, they would have three more children, for a total of three boys and a girl. Cube likes being a father. "The best thing about fatherhood is that you can look at all the mistakes you made and lay down a blueprint for your kids," he says. "I'm the firm but fair type. I'm cool and understanding, but there are rules," he adds. "Bottom line is that I respect my kids. A lot of parents want to be dictators around the house, which isn't me. I'm also not friends with my kids. I'm clearly

Director Brian Levant gives some pointers on the set of Are We There Yet? *For this family comedy, Cube had to learn how to ride a mechanical horse as well as a real one.*

in charge, but I do listen to opinions. That's all any kid wants. They want their words to be heard."

Throughout the 1990s, Cube kept more than busy playing a wide variety of movie roles. In 1995, he co-wrote and starred in the comedy *Friday.* In later years, it would be followed by the sequels *Next Friday* and *Friday After Next.* All three were quite popular with audiences who liked seeing the lighter side of Cube. "I like to do projects like *Friday* and stuff like that to kind of show the other side of who I am because I'm not serious 24 hours a day," he explains. "I have a sense of humor, it comes out every now and then."

> *"I'm not serious 24 hours a day," he explains. "I have a sense of humor, it comes out every now and then."*

In 1994, Ice Cube played Teddy Woods in the film *The Glass Shield,* then Fudge in 1995's *Higher Learning.* Just as people began to understand what kind of acting Cube was capable of, he startled movie fans by starring in the thriller *Anaconda.* And then, in his first leading role, he portrayed a South African man searching for his missing brother in *Dangerous Ground.* He was also executive producer on this movie.

In 1998, Ice Cube added to his list of professions by writing, directing, producing, and starring in *The Players Club.* He ended the decade by playing a soldier at the end of the Gulf War in *Three Kings.* He also had the part of Slink in the independent movie *Thicker Than Water.*

Not all of his acting or his movies were reviewed positively. Cube did not let bad reviews upset him, though. "You can't care about that stuff," he says. "It's like, first the public loves you, then they're sick of you, then you spring back again. You're always falling on and off the radar."

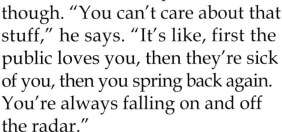

"I just want to do a lot of good projects. I just want it to be that when you see the Ice Cube name, it's worth your time to check it out."

When asked why he took such a wide variety of roles, Cube says, "I just want to do a lot of good projects. I just want it to be that when you see the Ice Cube name, it's worth your time to check it out. . . . These movies are going to be here when I'm gone, so I need to be proud of every single one because you can't erase them."

As busy as he's been as an actor, Cube has had less time to be a musician. However, he still managed to hook up with WC and Mack 10 to form the group Westside Connection. In 1996, the group released *Bow Down,* and then another album, *Terrorist Threats,* in 2003. Meanwhile, in 1998, Cube released his first solo album in several years, *War and Peace, Vol. 1.*

Whether it was on the big screen or over the radio, Ice Cube had arrived.

Into the New Millennium

Since the year 2000, Ice Cube has been busier than ever. His musical and movie careers have continued to grow. In 2000, he released *War and Peace, Vol. 2.* He teamed up again with former NWA band member Dr. Dre to produce the single "Chin Check." Snoop Dogg replaced Eazy-E, who had died of AIDS in 1995. Although there was a lot of talk about NWA re-forming and producing an album, it never happened. Later that year, Cube also joined the *Up in Smoke* tour, featuring Dr. Dre and rap star Eminem.

The following year, Cube starred in another thriller, called *Ghosts of Mars.* After that came the comedy *All About the Benjamins;* another Friday movie; and the huge hit *Barbershop.* He landed a role in the 2004 action movie *Torque,* and then in the sequel *Barbershop 2: Back in Business.*

In 2005, Cube appeared in the family comedy *Are We There Yet?* It was his first movie to appeal directly to parents and children. He followed it up with *XXX: State of the Union*. In 2006, he released the CD *Laugh Now, Cry Later*. He also created a six-episode reality television show called *Black.White.* for FX. It was designed to explore the relationship between blacks and whites in modern culture.

That same year, Cube was honored for his involvement in helping the homeless and economically disadvantaged become self-sufficient through a program called Chrysalis. He received an award at the annual fund-raiser, the Butterfly Ball. He is proud of all that the program is doing and is glad to help. "Normally I'm a little skeptical about this stuff," he says, "but to go (to

One of Ice Cube's most cherished awards is from the Fourth Annual Butterfly Ball, where he was honored for his charity work with Chrysalis.

downtown L.A.) and see what they do, I'm glad to be part of it."

Other projects include the lead role in *Welcome Back, Kotter,* a remake of a 1970s television show that gave John Travolta his start; and a sequel to *Are We There Yet?* called *Are We Done Yet?*

Cube plans to keep acting and singing. He says he is "not as confident as I would like to be. As an actor, there's a lot still that I need to learn, a lot of things I need to develop. With every movie I do, I get a better comfort zone. . . . I'm starting to take acting as serious as I take records."

Cube has matured a lot since his early years in music and movies. He has a family now and a more mature outlook. "You start out wanting the fame, the money, the glamour," he admits, "but then when you get it, you start wanting other things." No matter what he is singing or what part he is playing, Cube is always honest. "Some mornings I wake up mad at the world," he says. "Some mornings, I wake up happy to be alive. But I'm always myself. I never put on fronts or acts for people."

Cube has not forgotten who O'Shea Jackson is. "I found my magic through music and later, movies," he says. "But what makes me any different from a kid

> "You start out wanting the fame, the money, the glamour, but then when you get it, you start wanting other things."

Ice Cube, who calls himself "an everyday dude," attends a basketball game with his youngest son. Even with his busy career as a musician and actor, Ice Cube makes time for his family.

growing up on the South Side of Chicago right now? I'm the same kid who sat in his bedroom dreaming big. I'm the same everyday dude who just wanted to get out of some circumstances and make it. It might sound trite, but if it could happen to me, it could happen to anybody. I'm just an everyday dude to this day."

CHRONOLOGY

1969	Born O'Shea Jackson in South Central Los Angeles on June 15
1979	Hears first rap song, "Rapper's Delight" by the Sugarhill Gang
1983	Begins writing rap songs
1984	Forms C.I.A.
1986	With Eazy-E and Dr. Dre, forms NWA
1987	Leaves Los Angeles to attend the Phoenix Institute of Technology in Arizona
1988	Earns a degree in Architectural Drafting and Design; NWA's *Straight Outta Compton* is released
1989	Breaks from NWA and moves to New York City
1990	First solo album debuts; first son, O'Shea Jackson Jr., is born
1991	Makes acting debut in *Boyz N the Hood*
1992	Marries Kimberly Jackson; they will have three more children
1995	Forms Westside Connection with Mack 10 and WC; cowrites first movie, *Friday*
1997	Serves as executive producer on *Dangerous Ground*
1998	Makes solo screenwriting and directing debut with *The Players Club*
2000	Goes on the *Up in Smoke* tour with Eminem and Dr. Dre
2005	Is awarded for his work helping the homeless through the Chrysalis program
2006	Hosts Spike TV's AutoRox awards; releases *Laugh Now, Cry Later*

DISCOGRAPHY

1988	*Straight Outta Compton* (with NWA)	1997	*Featuring . . . Ice Cube*
1990	*AmeriKKKa's Most Wanted*	1998	*War and Peace, Vol. 1*
1991	*Death Certificate*	2000	*War and Peace, Vol. 2*
1992	*Predator*	2001	*Greatest Hits*
1993	*Lethal Injection*	2003	*Terrorist Threats* (with Westside Connection)
1994	*Bootlegs and B-Sides*	2006	*Laugh Now, Cry Later*
1996	*Bow Down* (with Westside Connection)		

FILMOGRAPHY

1991	*Boyz N the Hood*	2000	*Next Friday*
1992	*Trespass*	2001	*Ghosts of Mars*
1994	*The Glass Shield*	2002	*All About the Benjamins*
1995	*Friday*		*Friday After Next*
	Higher Learning		*Barbershop*
1997	*Anaconda*	2004	*Torque*
	Dangerous Ground		*Barbershop 2: Back in Business*
1998	*The Player's Club*		
	I Got the Hook Up	2005	*Are We There Yet?*
1999	*Three Kings*		*XXX: State of the Union*
	Thicker than Water	2006	*Black. White.* (reality TV series)

FURTHER READING

If you enjoyed this biography of Ice Cube, you might also enjoy these other Hip-Hop Superstar biographies from Mitchell Lane Publishers:

Bow Wow   *Eminem*   *Eve*
Ja Rule   *Jay-Z*   *Missy Elliott*
Nelly   *Queen Latifah*   *P. Diddy*
50 Cent

Works Consulted

McIver, Joel. *Ice Cube: Attitude.* London, United Kingdom: Sanctuary Publishing, 2002.

Cohen, David S. "Charity Takes Wing: Butterfly Ball Benefit Offers Fun, Funds," April 13, 2005, http://www.variety.com/vstory/VR1117921045?categoryid=38&cs=1)

Daly, Sean. "The Warm and Fuzzy Side of Ice Cube," *The Washington Post,* January 19, 2005, http://www.washingtonpost.com/wp-dyn/articles/A19580-2005Jan18.html

Fuchs, Cynthia. "Rapping Is Good Therapy: Interview with Ice Cube," January 28, 2005, http://www.popmatters.com/music/interviews/ice-cube-050128.shtml

Harris, Chris. "'Welcome Back, Ice Cube' — Rapper Taking on 'Kotter' Role," March 14, 2006, http://www.mtv.com/movies/news/articles/1526043/story.jhtml

"Ice Cube," Interview with *Teen Ink,* Rap News Network, posted March 2, 2005, http://www.rapnews.net/0-202-260108-00.html?tag=relnav

"Ice Cube Biography," http://www.icecube.org/bio.php

Ivey, Michael. "Ice Cube Produces Race-Conscious Reality Show," December 11, 2005, http://www.nobodysmiling.com/hiphop/news/85492.php

Pearlman, Cindy. "Ice Cube Warms Up for Family Fun," *Chicago Sun-Times,* January 16, 2005, http://www.suntimes.com/output/movies/sho-sunday-cube16.html

Star Pulse: "Ice Cube", http://www.starpulse.com/Music/Ice_Cube/index.html

Topel, Fred. "Ice Cube on *Torque* and *XXX2*," http://actionadventure.about.com/cs/weeklystories/a/aa011104.htm

INDEX